Macmillan/McGraw-Hill

Treasures

Online Interactive Student Book

www.macmillanmh.com

LOG ON ▶ **StudentWorks** *Plus*
Interactive Student Book

VIEW IT 👁

- Preview weekly concepts and selections

READ IT 📖

- Word-by-Word Reading

LEARN IT 🖱

- Comprehension Questions
- Research and Media Activities
- Grammar, Spelling, and Writing Activities

FIND OUT ↖

- Summaries and Glossary in other Languages

LOG ON ▶ **Online Activities**
www.macmillanmh.com

- **Interactive activities** and **animated lessons** for guided instruction and practice

IWB Interactive White Board Ready!

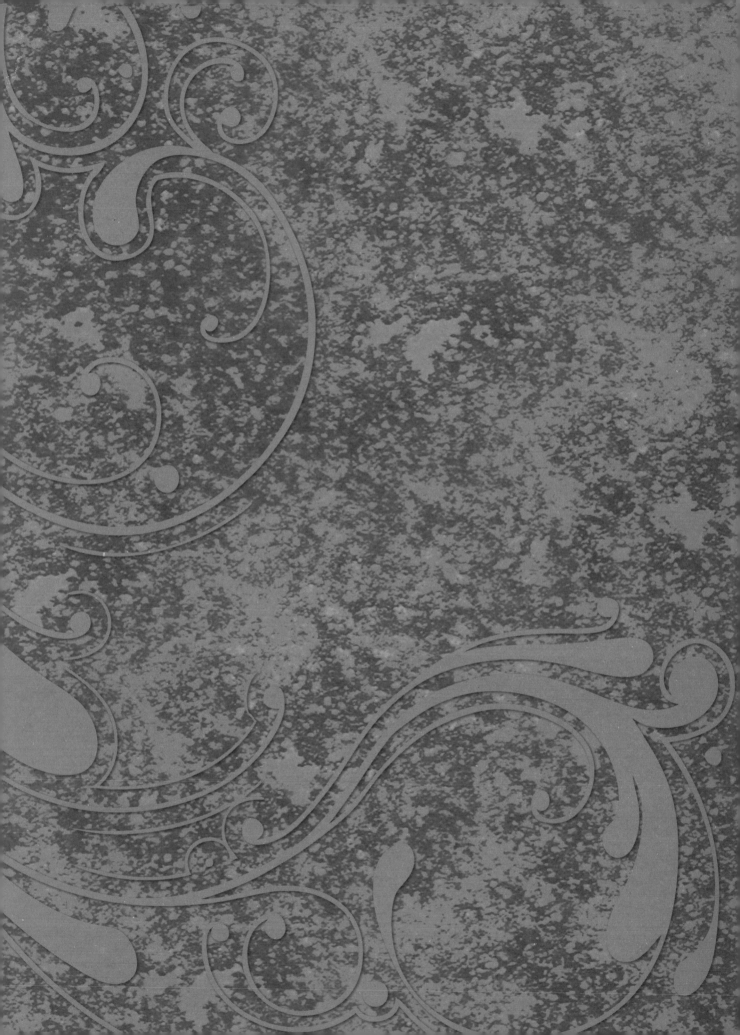

Treasures

A Reading/Language Arts Program

Macmillan/McGraw-Hill

Contributors

Time Magazine, Accelerated Reader

 RFB&D
learning through listening

Students with print disabilities may be eligible to obtain an accessible, audio version of the pupil edition of this textbook. Please call Recording for the Blind & Dyslexic at 1-800-221-4792 for complete information.

B

The McGraw·Hill Companies

Macmillan/McGraw-Hill

Published by Macmillan/McGraw-Hill, of McGraw-Hill Education, a division of The McGraw-Hill Companies, Inc., Two Penn Plaza, New York, New York 10121.

Printed in the United States of America

ISBN: 978-0-02-201726-2
MHID: 0-02-201726-7

2 3 4 5 6 7 8 9 DOW 13 12 11 10

Treasures

A Reading/Language Arts Program

Program Authors

Diane August

Donald R. Bear

Janice A. Dole

Jana Echevarria

Douglas Fisher

David Francis

Vicki Gibson

Jan E. Hasbrouck

Scott G. Paris

Timothy Shanahan

Josefina V. Tinajero

Macmillan/McGraw-Hill

Unit 2

Social Studies

Our Families, Our Neighbors

The Big Question

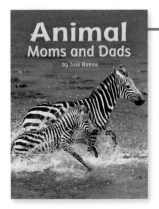

THEME: Animal Families

THEME: Helping Out

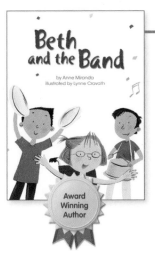

Show What You Know • REVIEW

Unit 2
Our Families, Our Neighbors

The **Big** Question

How do families and neighbors help one another?

_____

Theme Video
Our Families, Our Neighbors
www.macmillanmh.com

LOG ON ▶ VIEW IT

3

How do families and neighbors help one another?

How do you help your family? How do they help you? You may set the table. Your parents may read to you or make you a snack. Neighbors help, too. The crossing guard helps you cross the street. Mail carriers bring mail. Lots of people help you. You help them, too!

Research Activities

Make a neighborhood mural. Draw neighborhood places on the mural. Then draw a person who helps you. Cut out the person. Paste your person on the mural.

Keep Track of Ideas

As you read, use the **Four-Door Foldable** to draw and write about your family and neighbors. Draw a person and show how he or she helps. You can include places, too.

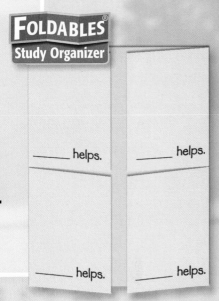

FOLDABLES®
Study Organizer

_____ helps.   _____ helps.

_____ helps.   _____ helps.

Digital Learning

StudentWorks _Plus_

Interactive Student Book

- **Research Roadmap**
  Follow a step-by-step guide to complete your research project.

Online Resources

- Topic Finder and Other Research Tools
- Videos and Virtual Field Trips
- Photos and Drawings for Presentations
- Related Articles and Web Resources
- Web Site Links

People and Places

Johnny Appleseed

Johnny Appleseed is known for planting the first apple trees in many areas of the United States when our country was young. His real name was John Chapman.

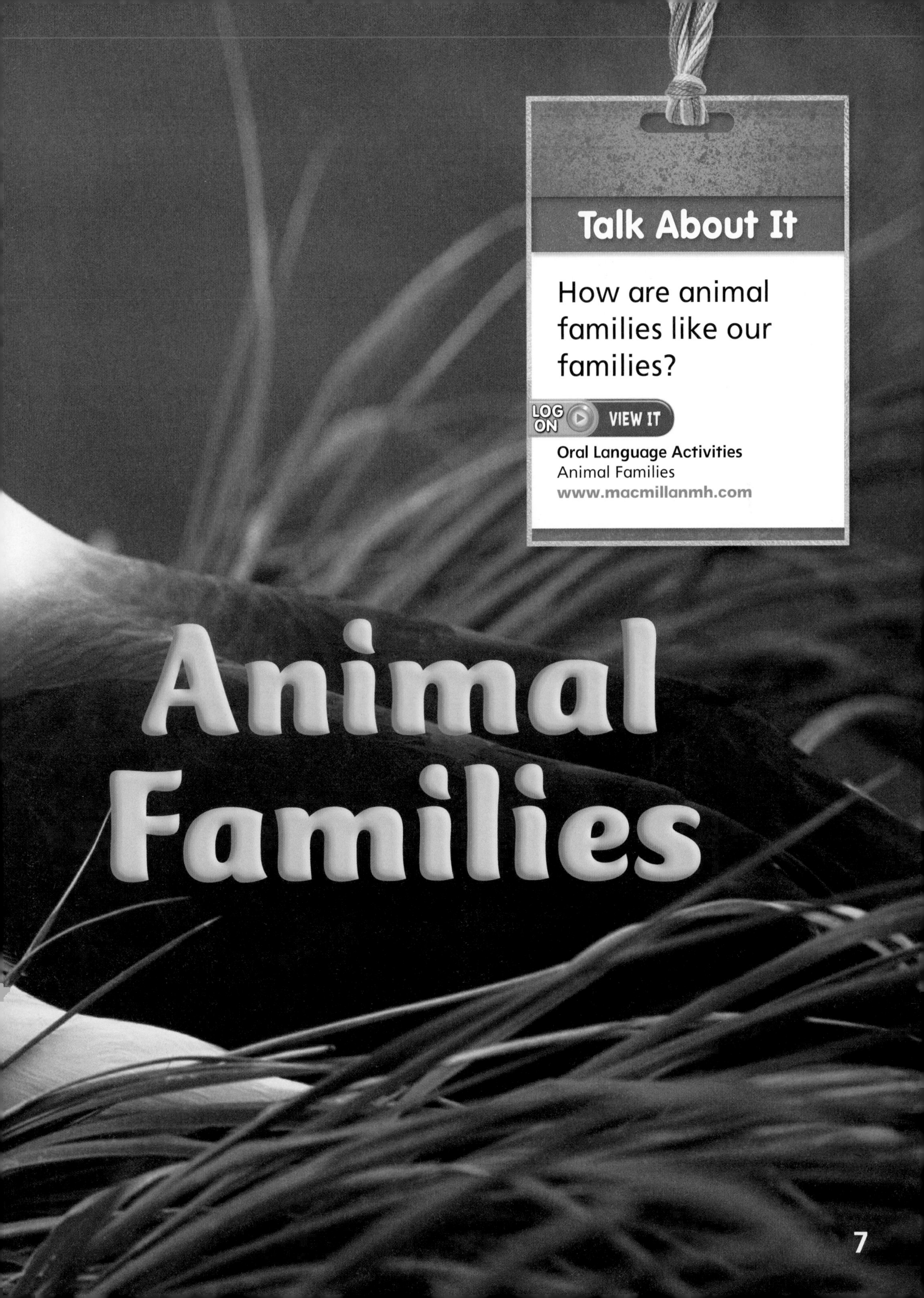

Talk About It

How are animal families like our families?

LOG ON VIEW IT

Oral Language Activities
Animal Families
www.macmillanmh.com

Animal Families

Our Mom and Dad

We are **two** cats.
We are not very big.

Our mom is a big cat.
Look at **her** jump!

Dad is big.
Dad runs a lot.
Dad is fast!

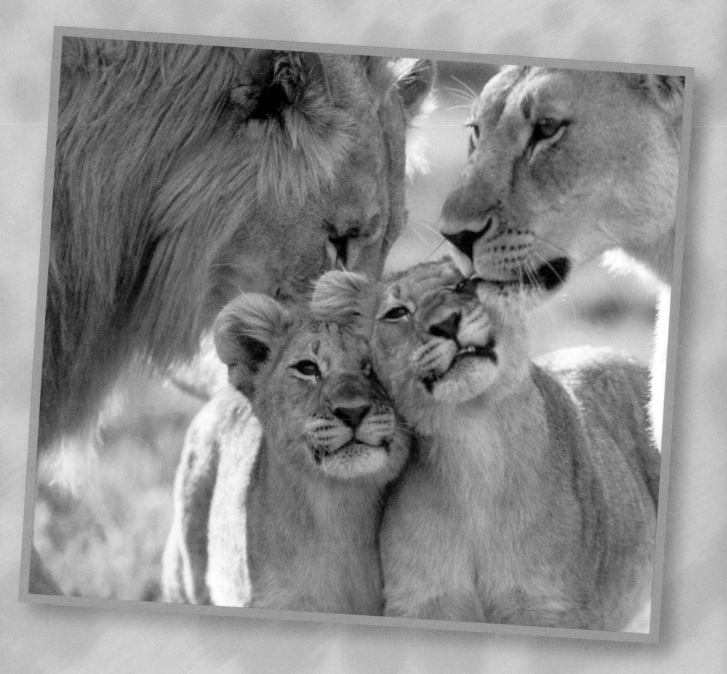

They are back.
We are glad!

Genre

Nonfiction gives information about a topic.

Summarize

Main Idea and Details

Use your Main Idea and Details Chart.

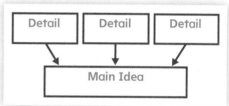

Read to Find Out

What do animal moms and dads do?

Animal
Moms and Dads

by Jose Ramos

What do animal moms do?
They do a lot.

What do animal dads do?
They do a lot, too.

My mom has food.
It is very good!

My dad got food.
Dad and I like it a lot.

My mom licks and licks.
I am clean.

My dad picks and picks.
I am clean.

Mom and I will hop, hop, hop.
I am in **her** sack.

My dad has a big back.
I can sit on top!

Look at **our** mom and dad.
It is a job for **two**.

We are in it.
Good job, Mom and Dad!

What can moms and dads do?

Moms and dads can play, too!

Meet Jose Ramos

Jose Ramos says, "When I was young, my dad took me to the zoo. I wanted to take a photo of every monkey! Today I'm a dad. I take my kids to the zoo. I like to help children learn about animals."

✔ Author's Purpose

Jose Ramos wants the reader to learn about animals. Draw an animal with its mom and dad. Write about it.

LOG ON ▶ FIND OUT

Author Jose Ramos
www.macmillanmh.com

✔ Comprehension Check

Retell the Selection

Use the Retelling Cards to retell the selection in order.

Retelling Cards

Think and Compare

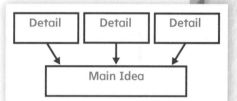

Detail	Detail	Detail
	Main Idea	

1. How are the bird parents helping their babies?

2. How do animal moms and dads clean their babies?

3. What is this selection mainly about? What details tell more about the main idea?

4. How is *Animal Moms and Dads* like "Our Mom and Dad"? How is it different?

Poetry

Genre

In a **Poem**, words are often put together so that they are fun to say.

Literary Elements

Rhythm Poems are written so that the words have a certain beat when you say them aloud.

Rhyme Words that rhyme end in the same sounds.

LOG ON ▶ **FIND OUT**

Poetry Rhythm and Rhyme
www.macmillanmh.com

Over in the Meadow

An Old Counting Rhyme

Over in the meadow,
In the sand in the sun,
Lived an old mother turtle
And her little turtle one.
"Dig," said the mother.
"I dig," said the one.
So they dug all day
In the sand in the sun.

29

Over in the meadow,
Where the stream runs blue,
Lived an old mother fish
and her little fishes two.

"Swim," said the mother.
"We swim," said the two.
So they swam all day
Where the stream runs blue.

Over in the meadow,
In the wide oak tree,
Lived an old mother owl
And her little owls three.
"Whoo," said the mother.
"Whoo, Whoo," said the three.
So they whooed all night
In the wide oak tree.

Connect and Compare

- What words in this poem rhyme?
- What words and word parts do you emphasize when you say the poem aloud?

Write About Families

Sam wrote about what some families do.

What Families Do

Families can help each other.

Families can play together.

Your Turn

Think about families you know.

Write about how families take care of each other.

Grammar and Writing

- Read Sam's writing.
  Point to the **noun** in each sentence.
  Point to each punctuation mark.

- Check your writing.
  Did you write about what families do?
  Does each sentence have a **noun**?

- Read your writing to a partner.

Helping Out

Talk About It

How do you help? What jobs do you like to do?

LOG ON ▶ VIEW IT

Oral Language Activities
Helping Out
www.macmillanmh.com

37

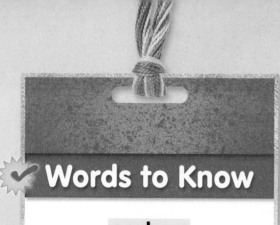

Who Will Help?

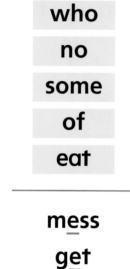

Words to Know

who
no
some
of
eat

mess
get

Read To Find Out
Will the mess get
cleaned up?

"Look at this mess," said Ben.
"**Who** will help?"

38

"We have **no** mops," said Jen.
"We have no bags," said Tim.

39

Comprehension

Genre
A Folktale is a story that has been told for many years.

Summarize
✔ Retell

Use your Retelling Chart.

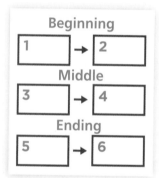

Read to Find Out
How does Little Red Hen make bread?

Little Red Hen

retold by Cynthia Rothman
illustrated by David Diaz

Award
Winning
Illustrator

Little Red Hen had a bit **of** wheat.
"**Who** will help plant?" asked Hen.

"Not I," said Dog.
"Not I," said Pig.
"Not I," said Cat.

"I will go to the well," said Hen.
"Who will help get **some** water?"

"Not I," said Cat.
"Not I," said Dog.
"Not I," said Pig.

"This is a big job," said Hen.
"Who will help get the wheat?"

"Not I," said Cat.
"Not I," said Dog.
"Not I," said Pig.

"I will mix and mix," said Hen.
"Who will help mix?"

"Not I," said Cat.
"Not I," said Dog.
"Not I," said Pig.

"Come quick!" said Hen.
"Look at this bread!"

"This is the best bread," said Hen.
"Who will help me **eat** some?"

"Let me," said Pig.
"Let me," said Cat.
"Let me," said Dog.

"**No**! No!" said Hen.
"This is a job for me!"

David Diaz's Job

David Diaz says, "I remember drawing a face on a worksheet when I was in first grade. I knew then that drawing was what I wanted to do when I grew up."

Other books by David Diaz

Illustrator David Diaz
www.macmillanmh.com

Illustrator's Purpose

David Diaz drew funny animals. Draw and write about one of the animals.

✔ Comprehension Check

Retell the Story

Use the Retelling Cards
to retell the story in order.

Retelling Cards

Think and Compare

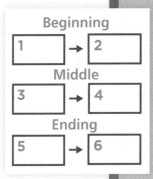

Beginning
| 1 | → | 2 |

Middle
| 3 | → | 4 |

Ending
| 5 | → | 6 |

1. Who are Little Red Hen's
   friends?

2. What does Little Red Hen do
   to make bread?

3. Why doesn't Little Red Hen share
   the bread? How have you acted
   in a similar situation?

4. How are Little Red Hen's
   friends different
   from the bears in
   "Who Will Help?"

57

From Wheat to Bread

Science

Genre
Nonfiction gives information about a topic.

✔ **Text Feature**
A Diagram is a picture that shows the parts of something.

Content Vocabulary
grow
kernels
factory

LOG ON ▶ FIND OUT

Science Growing Food
www.macmillanmh.com

How does wheat **grow**?
How do we use it?

Seeds

Wheat starts as a little seed.
Farmers plant the seeds.

59

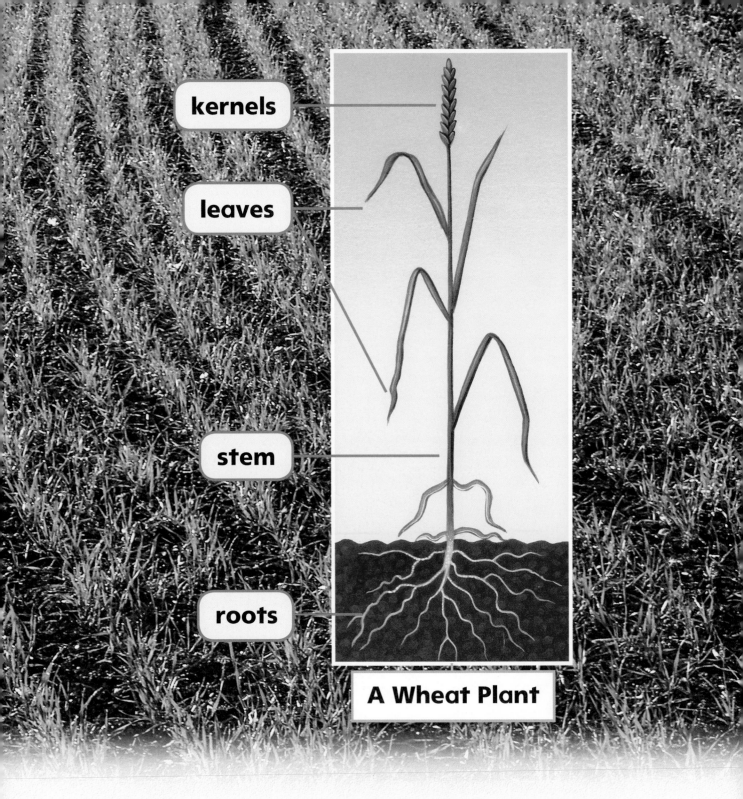

kernels

leaves

stem

roots

A Wheat Plant

The little plants have to get sun.
They have to get water.
They will grow to be big.

Now the wheat is tan.
The farmer picks off the **kernels**.
The kernels are good to eat.

The kernels go to a **factory**.
Here they are crushed.
The little bits of wheat are flour.

We use flour to make bread.
We use it in good things to eat.
That is what we do with wheat!

✔ Connect and Compare

- Who helps Little Red Hen make bread?
- How is bread made in "From Wheat to Bread"?
- What does the diagram tell you about wheat?

How to Make a Snack

Writing

✓ **Plural Nouns**

Add **-s** to make some nouns name more than one.

Eva wrote about how to make a snack.

How to Make a Snack

1. Get some nuts.

2. Get some grapes.

3. Mix and eat!

Your Turn

There are many kinds of sandwiches.

Think about a sandwich you like.

Tell how to make this sandwich.

Grammar and Writing

- Read Eva's How-To.
  Point to each plural noun.
  Tell a partner how to make Eva's snack.

- Check your How-To.
  Do your plural nouns end with an -s?
  Do you tell how to make the sandwich?

- Share your How-To with a partner.

Talk About It

Where do you live? What is your neighborhood like?

 **VIEW IT**

Oral Language Activities
Our Neighborhood
www.macmillanmh.com

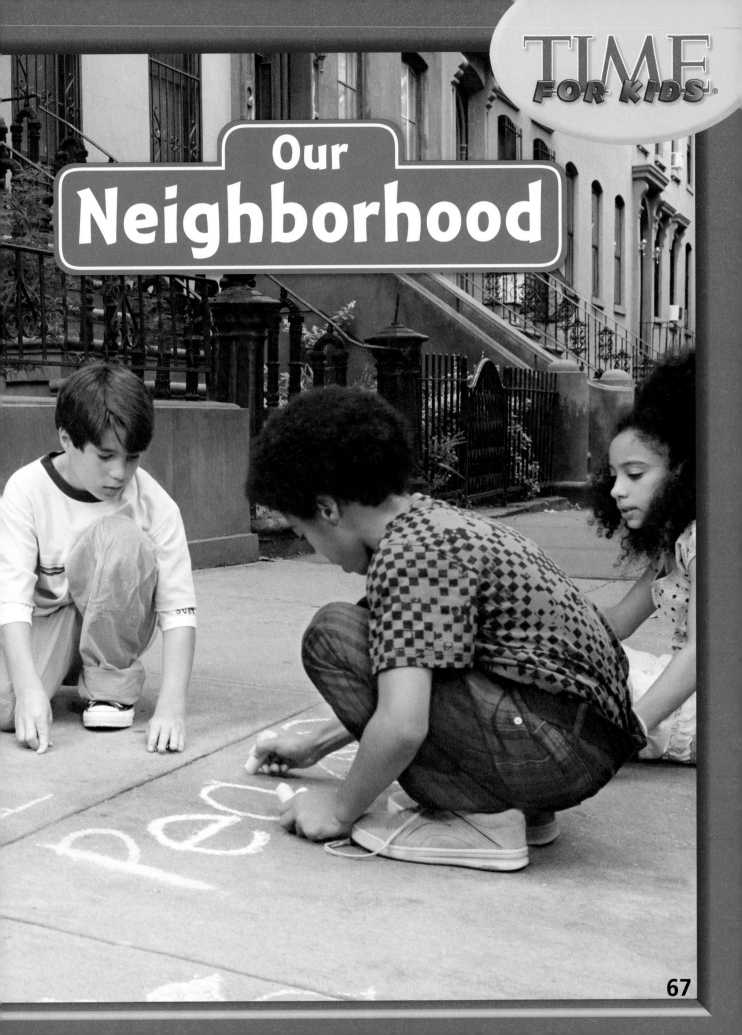

Our Neighborhood

live

place

many

out

_____

<u>g</u>rass

<u>st</u>ill

Come Out to Play!

I **live** in a big **place**.
It has lots of grass.

68

Many kids come out to play.
They are still here.
Come **out** to play!

On the Map

Greg and Stef **live** in a big town.

They go **out** a lot.

70

Here is the town on a map.

Greg and Stef go here a lot.
It is red. It has bricks.
It has **many** steps.
What is it?

Can you spot it on the map?

Greg and Stef like this
place a lot!
It has swings and sand.
What is it?

Can you spot it on the map?

Greg and Stef go here
to get stamps.
What is it?

Can you spot it on the map?

 Comprehension Check

Tell What You Learned

What did you learn about Greg and Stef's town?

Think and Compare

1. What is at the playground?

2. What places in the town do Greg and Stef go?

3. What can you learn about the town from looking at the map?

4. How are the places in "Come Out to Play!" and "On the Map" the same?

The Farmer's Market

Many kinds of food grow on a farm. Farmers pick the food when it's ripe.

Trucks take the food to the city. There it is sold at a farmer's market.

Farmers sell fruit, vegetables, and nuts. People come to buy farm-fresh food.

DIRECTIONS
Answer the questions.

1 **How do farmers get food to the city?**

(A) On bikes

(B) On planes

(C) On trucks

2 **What do farmers do at a farmer's market?**

(A) Buy seeds

(B) Grow nuts

(C) Sell food

3 **Why is the food at a farmer's market special?**

(A) It is sold.

(B) It is fresh.

(C) It is frozen.

Write About Your Neighborhood

Omar wrote about a park.

The writer added details.

My block is good for children.

The park has a very big slide.

Write to a Prompt

Think about your neighborhood.

Write a report about why your neighborhood is a good place to live.

Writing Hints

 Plan what you will say.

 Use complete sentences.

 Be sure your sentences make sense.

At Home

Talk About It

What is a home?

LOG ON ▶ **VIEW IT**

Oral Language Activities
At Home
www.macmillanmh.com

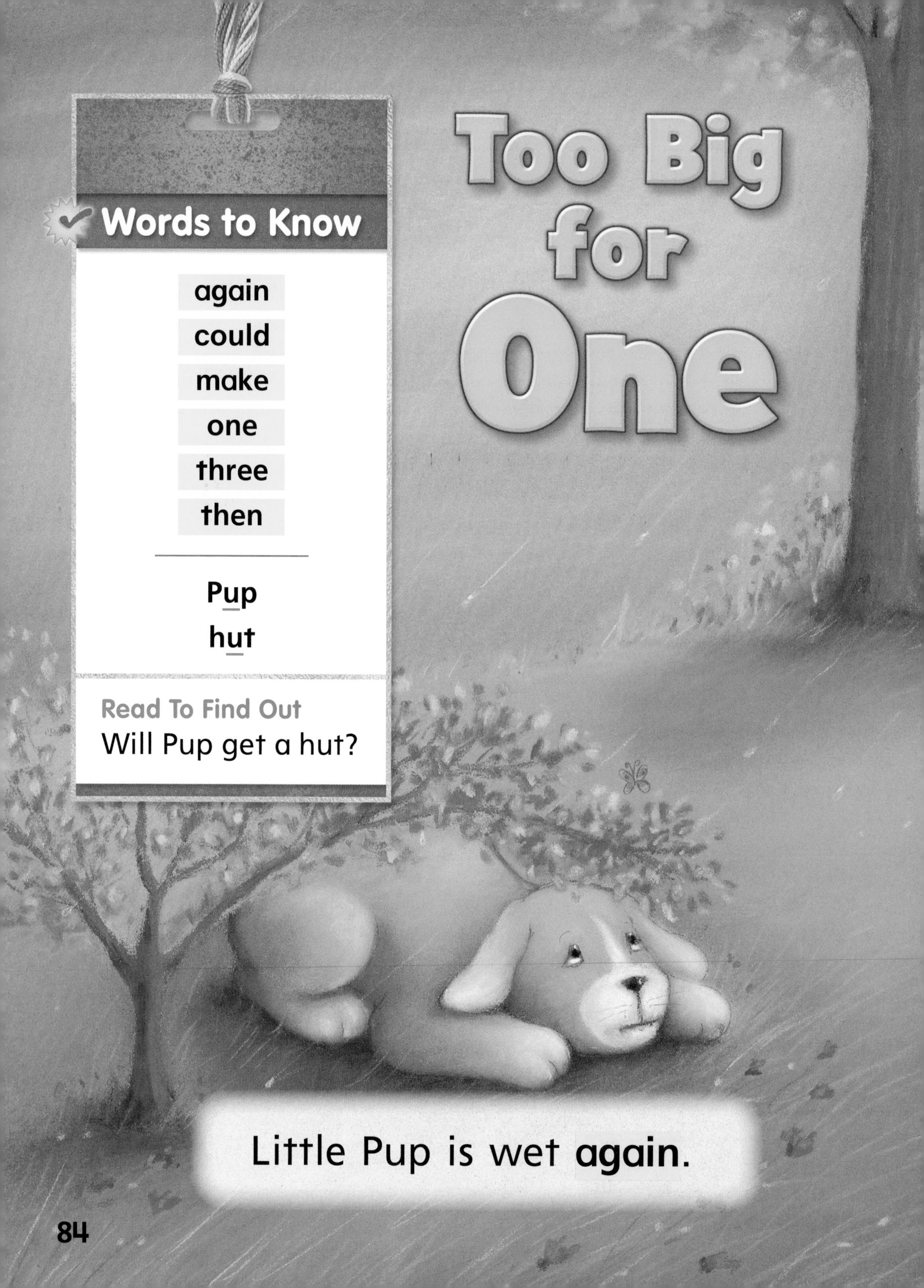

Too Big for One

Words to Know

again
could
make
one
three
then

Pup
hut

Read To Find Out
Will Pup get a hut?

Little Pup is wet **again**.

"We **could make** him a hut," said Pig.
"We could use sticks," said Cat.
"We could use bricks," said Pig.

85

They used sticks and bricks.
It was a very good hut!

"Is this too big for **one**?" asked Pup.
"It could fit **three**!" said Cat.
Then Pup said, "Come live with me!"
They did.

Comprehension

Genre
A Fantasy is a made-up story that could not really happen.

Visualize
✔ Plot
Use your Plot Chart.

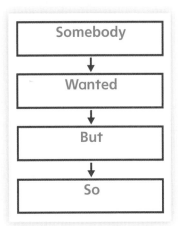

Somebody
↓
Wanted
↓
But
↓
So

Read to Find Out
What do the pigs do with the mud?

The Pigs, the Wolf, and the Mud

by Ellen Tarlow

illustrated by
Pablo Bernasconi

Award
Winning
Illustrator

Three little pigs lived in a mud hut.

"It is a mess," said Pig **One**.
"But pigs like a mess," said Pig Two.
"Mud is fun!" said Pig Three.

"Get this!" yelled Pig One.
She tossed mud to Pig Two.
"Mud is fun!" yelled Pig Three.

The bell rang.
"Little pigs, little pigs, let me in."

"It is the Big Bad Wolf!" said Pig One.
"We can not let you in," yelled the
pigs. "You will eat us up."

"Then I must huff and puff,"
said the wolf.
He huffed and huffed.
He puffed and puffed.

"Yuck!" said the wolf.
"I can not huff in this dust.
I can not puff in this dust."

The wolf rang the bell **again**.
"Little pigs, let me in!" he yelled.
"We will not let you in!" the pigs
yelled back.

"Then I must kick," said the wolf.
He kicked and kicked.

The hut fell in!

"Yuck!" said the wolf.

"Just look at this mud."

"You pigs are a big mess!"
"Yes!" yelled the pigs.
"Pigs like a big mess!"

"I do not!" yelled the wolf.
"I must get this mud off.
Good-bye, pigs."

"Let's **make** a hut," said Pig One.
"We **could** use bricks," said Pig Two.
"We could use sticks," said Pig Three.

"Let's use mud," said Pig One.
"Mud is best!" said Pig Two.
"Mud is fun!" said Pig Three.
"Yuck!" said the wolf.

Pablo's Place

Pablo Bernasconi loves illustrating animals doing funny things. Pablo's studio is a mess, full of junk and papers. But Pablo loves being surrounded by his things, just as the pigs in the story love being surrounded by mud.

Other books by Pablo Bernasconi

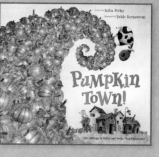

EL ZOO DE JOAQUIN

PUMPKIN TOWN!

LOG ON ▶ FIND OUT

Illustrator Pablo Bernasconi
www.macmillanmh.com

Illustrator's Purpose

Pablo Bernasconi loves his messy studio. Draw a place you love being. Write about this place.

✪ **Comprehension Check**

Retell the Story

Use the Retelling Cards
to retell the story in order.

Retelling Cards

Think and Compare

1. What do the pigs like?

2. What does the wolf do to
   get into the hut after he
   huffs and puffs?

3. What is the pigs' problem?
   How do they solve it?

4. How are the pigs
   like Pup in "Too Big
   for One"?

Somebody
↓
Wanted
↓
But
↓
So

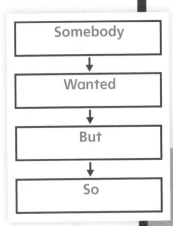

Social Studies

Genre
Nonfiction gives information about a topic.

✓ **Text Feature**
Photographs give more information about the text.

Content Vocabulary
homes
build
shelter

Social Studies Homes
www.macmillanmh.com

Homes Around the World

There are many kinds of **homes**. People **build** their homes to fit the place they live.

Look! This home was built into a cliff.

This is a good home for a wet place. There is a lot of water here. The stilts help keep this home dry.

This is a good home for a hot place. There is a lot of clay in this place. People use it to build homes. Clay keeps the home cool inside.

There is a lot of ice in this place. People can use it to build. This is an igloo. Igloos are good **shelter** from the cold.

What is your home like?

⭐ **Connect and Compare**

How are the igloo and the clay hut the same? How are they different? Use the photographs.

Neighborhood Fun

Talk About It

How do people in your neighborhood have fun together?

LOG ON ▶ **VIEW IT**

Oral Language Activities
Neighborhood Fun
www.macmillanmh.com

113

A Show

✔ **Words to Know**

want
put
show
together
under
all

Se<u>th</u>

si<u>ng</u>

Read To Find Out
What will the show be like?

Seth and Jill **want** to **put** on a **show**.
They tell lots of kids to come.

114

The kids want to see the show.
They sit **together** **under** a tent.

Seth jumps and sings.
Jill spins and taps.
They are very good!

All the kids like the show.
They clap and clap.
"Again!" they yell.

"Aunt Trish, look at that!" said Beth.

"What is it?" asked Aunt Trish.

120

"It is a band for kids," said Ann.

"We **want** to play in the band!"
said Beth, Bud, Ann, and Will.

"Can the kids **all** play?" asked Aunt Trish.

"Yes!" said a man in a red hat. "I am Shep. Make some instruments, kids."

"Make instruments?" asked the kids.

"Yes. Use the things in the box. It is **under** the bandstand," said Shep.

Rap
Tap
Tap

"I can hit this tub!" said Bud.
"It sounds just like a drum."
Rap! Tap! Tap!

"I can play this jug!" said Ann.
Hum! Hum! Hum!

Crish
Crush
Crash

"I can play the lids!" said Will.
Crish! Crush! Crash!

"What do you want to make, Beth?"
asked Aunt Trish.

"I just want to sing," said Beth.

"Can I sing in the **show**?" she
asked. "That will be fun for me."

"That will be fun for us, too,"
said the kids.

"Come on," said Will. "Sing with us!"

"Beth and the band will **put** on a show," said Shep.

"Yes!" yelled the kids.

"Let's all play **together**," said Shep.
"One, two, three! Play with me!"

Sing Along with Anne Miranda

Anne Miranda says, "When I was little, I sang in a group with my friend Elizabeth, her mother, and my neighbor Cathy, who was in high school. Once we were even on TV! We loved making music together, just like Beth and her friends."

Another book by Anne Miranda

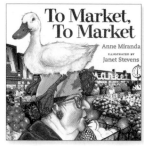

LOG ON ▶ FIND OUT

Author Anne Miranda
www.macmillanmh.com

✔ Author's Purpose

Anne Miranda wants to show that friends have fun making music. Draw your friends having fun. Write about it.

✔ Comprehension Check

Retell the Story

Use the Retelling Cards
to retell the story in order.

Retelling Cards

Think and Compare

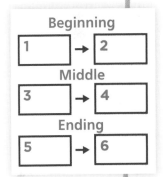

1. What do the kids see when they first get to the fair?

2. How do the kids get to be in the band?

3. How do the kids feel about being in the band?

4. How is the show in this story like the one in "A Show"?

135

Shake a Rattle!

Genre
Nonfiction can tell how to do or make something.

✔ **Text Feature**
Directions are the steps to follow to make something.

Content Vocabulary
instruments
rattles
music

 FIND OUT

Social Studies
Instruments Around the World
www.macmillanmh.com

What **instruments** do you see here? Shaking **rattles** is a fun way to make **music**.

136

Rattles can be big or little. They can be made of many things. Some have sand in them. Some have beans.

137

Do you want to make a rattle?
Here's how!

How to Make a Rattle

What You Need

plastic bottle

dried beans

stickers

What to Do

1 Put beans into the bottle.

2 Put fun stickers on.

3 Shake it and have fun!

Can you play the rattle loud? Can you play it soft? Can you make up a song?

⭐ **Connect and Compare**

How is a rattle like the instruments the kids made in *Beth and the Band*?

Write About Neighborhood Fun

✔ **Days of the Week**

The name of each **day** begins with a capital letter.

Leo wrote a story about a fun day.

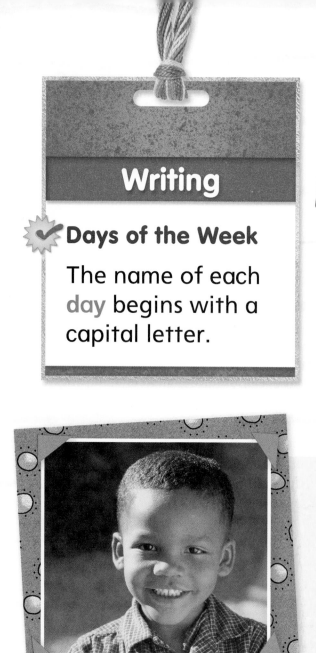

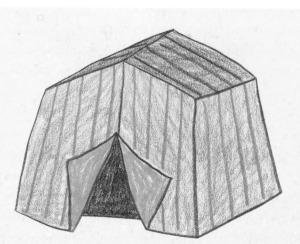

One Saturday, Jim and Ned put

up a big tent.

All the kids ate lunch in it.

140

Your Turn

Think of fun things kids could do in a neighborhood.

Write a story about it.

Name the characters. Name the day the fun thing takes place.

Grammar and Writing

- Read Leo's story.
  Point to the **day** of the week.
  Name the characters. Tell what they do.

- Check your story.
  Do your characters do something fun?
  Do **days** of the week and characters' names begin with capital letters?

- Read your story to a partner.

Review

Retell
Plot
Directions
Diagram

Frog Lost

"Frog is lost!" said Gus.

"I will help look," said Meg.

Gus looked under the bed.

Meg looked in her pack.

"What does Frog like to do?" asked Meg.

"She likes to get wet," said Gus.

Gus and Meg ran to the sink.

Frog sat on a dish, getting a drink!

READ TOGETHER

Make a Book!

What do you see outside your door?

Show what you see.

Make a book!

inside pages

front cover

back cover

My Book
by R.A. Cat

The diagram shows the parts of the book.

What You Need

- one sheet of paper
- crayons

What to Do

Read the directions.

1. Fold your paper.

2. Draw a door on your cover. Write **Outside My Door**.

Outside My Door

3. Turn the page. Draw three things outside your door.

4. Write about your pictures.

I see birds.   I see a tree.
I see houses.

5. Show your book to a friend!

Word Study

Person, Place, or Thing?

- Read the words below. Which name people? Which name places? Which name things?

  hat   man   mom   school   nut

- Think of more words that name people, places, and things. Work with a partner.

Common or Proper?

- Proper nouns name special people and places. They begin with a capital letter. Common nouns begin with a lower-case letter. Read the words.

  hat   dan   box   texas   pond

- Write them correctly on paper. Think of more proper and common nouns. Add them to your list.

Comprehension

Parts of a Book

- Use this book to study book parts. Work with a partner.

- Find the table of contents. Read the titles. Then find the page number.

- Go to each story. Use the page numbers. Read the author's and illustrator's names.

Act It Out

- Act out *The Pigs, the Wolf, and the Mud*.

- Work with a small group. One child can narrate the story. The others can read the dialogue.

- Add actions and more dialogue.

- Pay attention to the order of events as you act out the story.

Glossary

What Is a Glossary?

A glossary can help you find the meanings of words. The words are listed in alphabetical order. You can look up a word and read it in a sentence. There is a picture to help you.

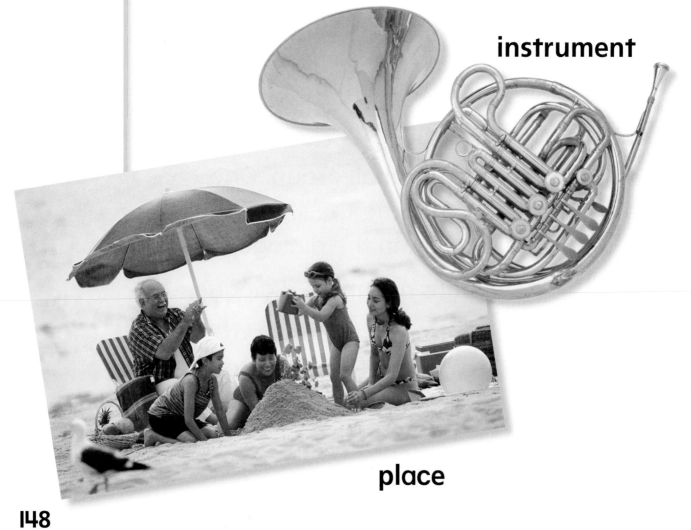

instrument

place

Sample Entry

Letter

H h

Main Entry

Hen

Sentence

A **hen** lays eggs.

tossed

149

Dd

drum

I play the **drum** in the band.

Ee

eat

I like to **eat** dinner with my family.

Hh

hen

A **hen** lays eggs.

Ii

instrument

This **instrument** makes a loud sound.

Jj

jug

The **jug** has milk in it.

Pp

place

The beach is a fun **place**!

152

Tt

tossed

Ms. Rapp **tossed** the ball to Rosa.

Ww

well

Sam got water from a **well**.

Acknowledgments

The publisher gratefully acknowledges permission to reprint the following copyrighted material:

"Over in the Meadow: An Old Counting Rhyme" by Olive A. Wadsworth. Copyright © 1991 by Scholastic Inc., 730 Broadway, NY, NY. Reprinted with permission of Scholastic Inc., NY.

Book Cover, TO MARKET, TO MARKET by Anne Miranda, illustrated by Janet Stevens. Text copyright © 1997 by Anne Miranda. Illustrations copyright © 1997 by Janet Stevens. Reprinted by permission of Harcourt Children's Books.

Book Cover, ROADRUNNER'S DANCE by Rudolfo Anaya, illustrated by David Diaz. Text copyright © 2000 by Rudolfo Anaya. Illustrations copyright © 2000 by David Diaz. Reprinted by permission of Hyperion Books for Children.

Book Cover, THE LITTLE SCARECROW BOY by Margaret Wise Brown, illustrated by David Diaz. Text copyright © 2005 by Margaret Wise Brown. Illustrations copyright © 2005 by David Diaz. Reprinted by permission of HarperTrophy.

ILLUSTRATIONS

Cover Illustration: Pablo Bernasconi

28–33: Krystina Stasiak. 38–41: Anna Vojtech. 42–57: David Diaz. 59-62: Tom Leonard. 71: Mircea Catusanu. 73: Mircea Catusanu. 75–76: Mircea Catusanu. 80: Mike Gordon. 84–87: Marisol Sarrazin. 88–105: Pablo Bernasconi. 110: Ken Bowser. 114–117: Laura Ovresat. 118–135: Lynn Cravath. 140–141: Daniel DelValle. 142–143: Stacy Schuett. 150, 152-153 Brian Karas.

PHOTOGRAPHY

All photographs are by Ken Cavanagh or Ken Karp for Macmillan/McGraw Hill (MMH) except as noted below:

iv: (t) Masterfile Royalty-Free; (c) Steve Bloom. v: Image Source/Getty Images. 2–3: Masterfile Royalty-Free. 4: Cathrine Wessel/Corbis. 4–5: D. Berry/PhotoLink/Getty Images. 5: the Granger Collection, New York. 6–7: Steve Bloom Images/ Alamy. 8: Anup Shah/Nature Picture Library. 9: Gabriela Staebler/zefa/Corbis. 10: David A. Northcott/Corbis. 11: Panthera Productions/Getty Images. 12–13: Steve Bloom. 14: Jean Michel Labat/Ardea London Ltd. 15: Art Wolfe/Photo Researchers. 16: Robert Maier/Animals Animals/Earth Scenes. 17: Tom & Pat Leeson/Photo Researchers. 18: Michel & Christine Denis-Huot/Photo Researchers. 19: Peter Lilja/Getty Images. 20: Tim Flach/Getty Images. 20–21: Joe McDonald/Corbis. 22–23: Peter Johnson/Corbis. 23: Inge Yspeert/Corbis. 24: Steve Bloom. 25: JM Labat/Peter Arnold. 26: (t) Courtesy Jose Ramos; (b) Art Wolfe/Photo Researchers. 27: Robert Maier/Animals Animals/ Earth Scenes. 34: Peter Beck/Corbis. 35: Marc Romanelli/Getty Images. 36–37: George Disario/Corbis. 56: Courtesy of David Diaz. 58–59: (t/bkgd) Image 100/Getty Images; (b/bkgd) Digital Vision Direct. 59: (c) AGStock USA/Alamy; (cr) C. Borland/PhotoLink/Getty Images. 60: John Prior Images/ Alamy. 61: (bkgd) Digital Vision Direct; (inset) JW/Masterfile. 62: (t) Larry Lefever/Grant Heilman Photography; (l) Michael Newman/Photo Edit; (cl) Stock Food/SuperStock. 63: Brand X Pictures/Alamy. 64: Tony Anderson/Getty Images. 65: Michael Newman/Photo Edit. 66–67: Image Source/Getty Images. 68: RicPeterson/Alamy. 69: DCA Productions/Getty Images. 70: Tony Freeman/Photo Edit. 72: Swerve / Alamy. 74: Andrea Rugg/Beateworks/Corbis. 76: Bruce Clarke/Index Stock. 78: Jeff Greenberg/Photo Edit. 79: (l) Bill Aron/Photo Edit; (c) Rainer Dittrich/Getty Images; (r) Car Culture/Getty Images. 80: LWA-Sharie Kennedy/Corbis. 81: Bet Noire/Shutterstock . 82–83: Adam Tanner/The Image Works. 104: Courtesy of Natalia Berdini. 106: Mediacolor's/Alamy. 107: Upperhall Ltd./Robert Harding World Imagery/Corbis. 108: Stone/Getty Images. 109: Bryan & Cherry Alexander Photography. 110: Roy Morsch/AGE Fotostock. 111: Design Pics Inc/Alamy. 112–113: ColorBlind Images/Getty Images. 134: Courtesy Anne Miranda. 136: (cr) Canadian Museum of Civilization/Corbis; (bl) David Young-Wolff/Photo Edit; (bc) AllOver Photography/Alamy; (br) Royalty-Free/CORBIS. 137: (c) AP Images/Pat Vasquez-Cunningham; (br) Dynamic Graphics Group/Creatas/Alamy. 138–139: Ken Karp/Macmillan McGraw-Hill. 140: David Schmidt/ Masterfile. 144: Thinkstock/Getty Images. 145: Stockdisc/ PunchStock; (bc) Macmillan/McGraw-Hill. 146: Nic Hamilton/ Alamy. 148: (cr) C Squared Studios/Getty Images; (bl) Jeff Zaruba/Corbis. 149: (t) Robert Maier/Animals Animals; (b) Bananastock/Alamy. 150: Ariel Skelley/Corbis. 151: (t) Robert Maier/Animals Animals; (b) C Squared Studios/Getty Images. 152: Jeff Zaruba/Corbis. 153: Bananastock/Alamy.